this very moment

will never come again

this breeze, this cricket's song

this you, this me

ISBN 978-0-9977956-8-4

Copyright © 2025 by Kathleen Kramer

All rights reserved.

Books are available through the publisher and amazon.com, as well as bookstores in the Ithaca, NY area.

Credits:

All of the photos appearing in *this very moment* were captured by the author, **Kathleen Kramer,** with the exception of the author photo lovingly taken by her husband Jack as well as the candid of Kathy and Jack on page 351 taken by their dear friend Betsy Bobo.

Cover and book design/layout by E. Nan Edmunds, lifelong friend and occasional confidante of the author.

this very moment...

A collection of poems

and the photos that inspired them

by

Kathleen Kramer

Author's Notes

This is a book composed of small moments: each one consists of a photo and a small poem. When each is viewed through the lens of the reader's heart, it is my hope that it will open into a larger moment, rich with personal meaning.

This way of thinking—that the moment holds limitless meaning—was a gift from my parents. In western Pennsylvania, in the 1940s and 50s, the door to outdoors was opened for the five of us by our father and his love for all things found there.

One long-ago moment has stayed with me for 70 years. It was early spring and Dad took me on a tiny adventure to a roadside bank still damp and layered with last fall's leaves. He bent down and with careful fingers brushed them aside.

"There," he said, almost whispering. "Trailing Arbutus."

At first, I didn't see it. It was so small and seemingly unimpressive until Dad pinched off one hairy stem and handed it to me to smell. How do you describe a fragrance? Only by likening it to another. And try as I might, I still can't think of anything that smells as spring-like, as rare, as that cluster of tiny pink blossoms.

Our mother had a love of color—a love that, sadly, was being challenged by encroaching blindness. Once, when I was in my late

teens, I was driving her to an appointment, and she suddenly said, "Kathy, look! Look at the yellow trees on that hillside!" Like many young people, I was probably focused on my own thoughts or on the music from the car radio  and was somewhat oblivious to the autumn beauty. Then she added, quietly, "Yellow is the only color I can still see."

For all these intervening years—sixty, at least—color has called to me, often in my mother's voice, "Kathy, look!"

My guess is that you, the reader, also have a lifetime of such happenings that have shaped the gifts you have to share. It is my hope that this book of small poems can be a tribute to life's small moments—moments that have taken on enhanced value, moments burnished by the understanding that, as we age, each one holds the potential to be the ultimate moment.

As seen through the eyes of an elder in a culture now shaped by the young, may these photos and the tiny poems that accompany them help you savor *this very moment*.

Offerings

this very moment 13	after weeks of rain 99
altar of twigs 17	outside my window 103
answered prayer 21	one o'clock 107
family portrait 25	the plight of the larch 111
a flower girl 29	this sunshiny morning 115
a friend, a scone 33	the setting sun 119
i walk alone 35	under each tree 123
in the cemetery 39	a moon so bright 127
blowing against my window 43	the silence of darkness 131
sunny morning 47	i'm learning the names 133
one by one by one 49	today i found myself 137
tonight's full moon 53	an ordinary wednesday 141
every morning 57	for the believer 145
early morning 61	summer solstice 149
today, god is working 65	crossing the evening sky 153
pillows in the pasture 69	twilight's blue light 157
a long full day 73	honey for sale 161
ice cream, hot fudge 77	late summer, late evening 165
the sun is shining 81	last year's petunias 169
wanting nothing 83	just past midnight 173
like beaded curtains 87	light through broken walls 177
marguerite daisy 91	beautiful 181
my aging life grows smaller 95	i can no longer care 185

from the prow 189	*some tears* 281
needing comfort 193	*today, needing to be empty* 285
one silver drop 197	*a toast to daylight* 289
at last i know 201	*under the bird feeder* 293
in the cemetery 205	*these days, it's the small things* .. 297
window becomes mirror 209	*outside inside* 301
if color had voice 213	*lowes' forevergreen forest* 305
at the cemetery 217	*under the dish towels* 309
tulip poplar 221	*my mug for morning* 311
becoming old 225	*two winter willows* 315
little bowl of light 229	*this clear winter night* 319
little dogwood 233	*bare black branches* 321
maundy thursday's moon 237	*in the black bowl of sky* 325
my woods 241	*sometimes color blooms* 329
be still 245	*to the west* 333
carefully, the tree spreads 249	*empty bowl* 337
balancing the moon 253	*my dear one is sick* 341
twilight 257	*so old* 343
the perfection 261	*so fragile* 347
the harder i try 265	*so many years* 351
skylight frame 269	
among the bare trees 273	
every leaf, every line 277	

this very moment...

this very moment
will never come again —
this breeze, this cricket's song
this you, this me

this very moment...

17

altar of twigs
scrap of sunlight
. . . it is enough

this very moment...

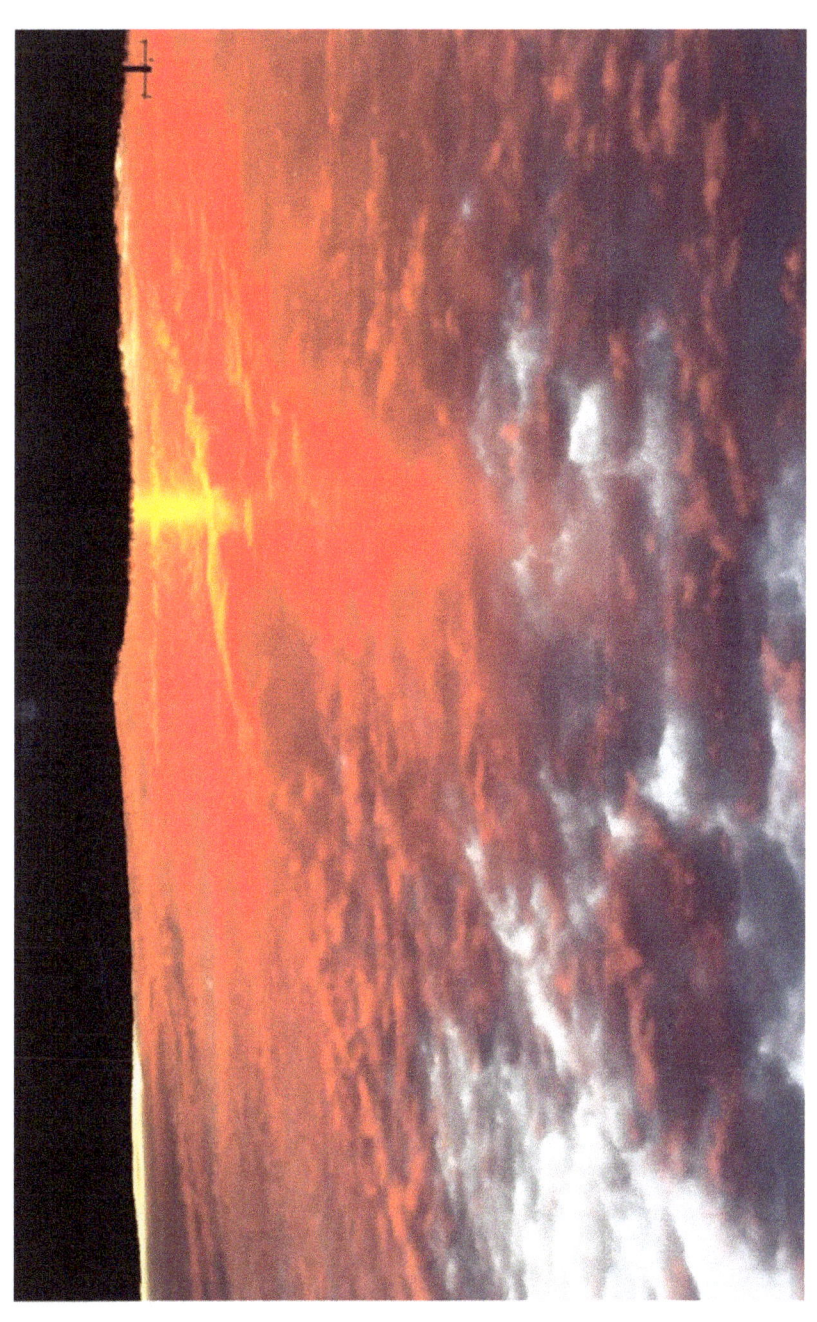

answered prayer
may require
only that we stop to see

This family portrait was created by Needle Felting Artist, Shelly Ditty. Shelly is a new-found cousin—thanks to Ancestry.com—and her diligence in seeking out her lost family has been a treasured gift to me, as has this beautiful family portrait. Shelly has imbued these little representations with a warmth that emanates from them every time I gaze at them, remembering blessed times. Thank you, Shelly.

family portrait
grandpap   mama   me
and the truck

this very moment...

a flower girl
among the taller guests . . .
the dogwood blooms

a friend, a scone
a cup of tea —
a poem without words

this very moment...

i walk alone
and find
my self

this very moment...

in the cemetery
each gravestone
makes its own shadow

this very moment...

blowing against my window
raindrops and pear blossoms
april!

sunny morning
a butterfly's shadow
floats by at my feet

this very moment...

one by one by one
a bee samples each petal
bergamot buffet!

this very moment...

tonight's full moon
makes everything seem important
makes everything seem unimportant

this very moment...

every morning
the fragrance of tea …
those breakfasts with dad

this very moment...

early morning
our red maple offers
her spring bouquet

this very moment...

today, god is working
on his book for babies—
CLOUDS, he writes

this very moment...

pillows in the pasture
ahh . . . the sheep
are lying down

this very moment...

a long full day—
at the end
a red balloon

this very moment...

ice cream hot fudge
whipped cream cherry
my therapy for today

the sun is shining
i saw it through the feathers
of a small brown bird

this very moment...

wanting nothing
gives me
everything

this very moment...

like beaded curtains
blossoms sway in the breeze
quietly, evening comes

this very moment...

marguerite daisy
shyly lifts her pure white skirts
underneath, a blue surprise!

this very moment...

my aging life grows smaller—
little joys become
big joys

from one year ago —
the message is still the same —
only more so

this very moment...

after three weeks of rain
three cups of sunlight to share
whom shall we invite?

this very moment...

outside my window
yellow petunias . . .
sunshine every day!

this very moment...

one o'clock
this easter morning
an egg-shaped moon

this very moment...

the plight of the larch
deciduous coniferous
both yet neither!

this very moment...

115

this sunshiny morning
the very air is perfumed
with dandelions!

this very moment...

119

the setting sun
spotlights the little dogwood
in her summer dress

this very moment...

under each tree
a quiet pool of darkness —
evening comes again

this very moment...

a moon so bright
the stars
cover their eyes!

the silence of darkness
suddenly broken —
firefly gossip

this very moment...

*i'm learning the names
of wildflowers
so i'll always be*

*surrounded
by
friends*

this very moment...

today i find myself
smiling at the clouds
the way they change

this very moment...

an ordinary wednesday
except for these purple leaves
and the burial of my father

this very moment...

for the believer
there is no such
thing as alone

this very moment...

summer solstice
again i lift my old face
to the old sun

this very moment...

crossing the evening sky
half moon gets tangled
among the branches

this very moment...

twilight's blue light
white petals
even whiter

this very moment...

honey for sale
the honor system
sweet!

this very moment...

late summer, late evening
at last, the fragrance
of these blue-eyed daisies

this very moment...

last year's petunias
last year's moon
this year's memory

this very moment...

just past midnight
my 80th birthday
a full moon, waning

this very moment...

light through broken walls
smell of dusty hay
my grandmother's voice

this very moment...

beautiful . . .
and yet prickly
we all know someone

this very moment...

i can no longer care
for a plant i've loved
so today i gave him away
and wept

this very moment...

from the prow
of my house
i set sail at sunrise

this very moment...

needing comfort
i remember
my father's hand

this very moment...

one silver drop . . .
then two!
oh we need this rain!

this very moment...

at last i know
what holds up the heavens . . .
it's this dogwood

this very moment...

in the cemetery
amidst the many tombstones
an old tree celebrates life

this very moment...

window becomes mirror
do trees know
how beautiful they are?

this very moment...

if color had voice
this green
would sing soprano!

this very moment...

at the cemetery
leaves change
all else remains the same

this very moment...

tulip poplar
has shed her red dress
graceful limbs free till spring

this very moment...

becoming old
slow ... slow ... slow
fast!

this very moment...

little bowl of light last rose of sharon

this very moment...

little dogwood
wears her second best dress
for fall

this very moment...

maundy thursday's moon
white as the bread
soon to be broken

this very moment…

my woods
even in the familiar
there is mystery

this very moment...

245

be still
better still
be the stillness

this very moment...

carefully, the tree spreads
her winter shadow on the ground
and waits for spring to dress her

this very moment...

balancing the moon
on his top most twig . . .
this tree wins the prize!

this very moment...

twilight—
leafy carpet welcomes
the twilight of the year

this very moment...

261

the perfection
of imperfection
... sycamores

this very moment...

the harder i try
not to care
the more i care

this very moment...

skylight frame—
black branches
silver rain

this very moment...

among the bare trees
she searches for me
here I am moon!

this very moment...

every leaf, every line
etched by the sharp breath
of winter

this very moment...

some tears are best cried alone

this very moment...

285

today, needing to be empty
i went to the lake and wept
until i was

this very moment...

a toast to daylight
tomorrow
4 seconds more

this very moment...

under the bird feeder
arthur murray's patterns
for the turkey trot!

this very moment...

these days, it's the small things—
like this little snowman—
that give delight to darkness

this very moment...

outside   inside
    light
brings them together

this very moment...

lowes's forevergreen forest
happily i lose
my way

under the dish towels
mother's stash
of caramels

this very moment...

my mug for morning tea
sports a spotted hen
i call her dottie

this very moment...

two winter willows
poised for the dance to begin ...
all they need is spring

this clear winter night
the air
smells of starlight

this very moment . . .

bare black branches
flocked with snow
but look, spring's buds are there!

this very moment...

in the black bowl of sky
a bright moon floats
among clabbered clouds

this very moment...

sometimes
color blooms
out of darkness

this very moment...

to the west
the clouds are clearing
my grip softens

this very moment...

empty bowl
filled with shadow
filled with light

my dear one is sick
can i turn worry
into prayer

this very moment...

so old
 so strong
  this friendship

this very moment...

so fragile
that place
where hearts touch

so many years

still . . .

there's this

About the Author

Kathleen Kramer's early years were spent in Pennsylvania's coal mining and farming region, where life was lived in the midst of a large extended family and influenced by the solidity of the earth and the rhythm of the seasons. At 19, she left for the city and spent five memorable years working in Washington, DC, for the Department of Defense. There followed a three-year stint in Maine where subsistence farming took her back to the land. New York State became the family's next home where Kathy and her husband Jack reared their three sons, Andrew, Ian, and Kyle, in Northport, a small historical village on Long Island Sound.

During that time and over a period of 10 years of balancing family, classes, and work, Kathy earned a BA at Empire State College and her MLS at Long Island University before moving to the Finger Lakes area of New York.

It was in the stunning setting of the gorges and lakes of Central New York that Kathy began to explore a long-deferred interest. Writing circles offered by Zee Zahava, beloved Ithaca writer and Poet Laureate of Tompkins County, opened the door to an adventure in creativity that has richly blessed Kathy's life. The 33 years that followed were filled with writing

and performing plays, participating in poetry critiquing groups, publishing her work in various literary journals, and presenting readings throughout the region.

Now, Kathy says she finds herself turning away from writing longer works and is discovering sudden inspiration and joy in writing small poems, like those in this book. As one's life, by necessity, narrows in scope, those gifts of nature and everyday life that are close at hand can be seen in a way that heightens their beauty and calls forth their often-profound meaning.

It is these small gifts that are offered in this book. Kathy says she is privileged to share them with you and she suggests that this is a book to be read slowly, one photo, one tiny poem at a time. As one poem says, *to be in the moment is to be in the eternal.*

—this very moment is Kathy's fourth full-length collection, preceded by

Boiled Potato Blues
2011

Planting Wild Grapes
2016

Everything Matters
2020